EMERGENCY!

OIL DISASTER

Jen Green

ARCTURUS

This edition first published in 2011 by Arcturus Publishing

Distributed by Black Rabbit Books
P.O. Box 3263
Mankato
Minnesota MN 56002

Printed in China

Library of Congress Cataloging-in-Publication Data

Green, Jen.
 Oil disaster / Jen Green.
    p. cm. -- (Emergency!)
 Includes index.
 ISBN 978-1-84837-955-8 (library binding)
 1. Oil spills--Juvenile literature. I. Title.
 TD427.P4G69 2012
 363.738'2--dc22

                            2011006645

Series concept: Alex Woolf
Editor and picture researcher: Alex Woolf
Designer: Ian Winton

Picture credits
Corbis: Corbis: 4 (Bob Fleumer), cover and 5 (Najiah Feanny), 6 (Jo Yong-Hak/Reuters), 7 (Lavandeira Jr/epa), 8 (Bettmann), 9 (Bettmann), 10 (Alain DeJean/Sygma), 11 (Richard Melloul/Sygma), 16 (Natalie Fobes/Science Faction), 18 (Natalie Fobes/Science Faction), 19 (Natalie Fobes), 20 (Peter Turnley), 21 (Robert van der Hilst), 22 (Matthew Polak), 23 (Chinch Gryniewicz/Ecoscene), 24–25 (US Coast Guard), 26 (Petty Officer 3rd Class Colin White/US Coast Guard), 27 (Christopher Berkey), 29 (Reuters).
Rex: 13 (Sipa Press), 14, 15 (Sipa Press).

Every attempt has been made to clear copyright. Should there be any inadvertent omission, please apply to the publisher for rectification.

Supplier 03, Date 0411, Print Run 1051
SL001700US

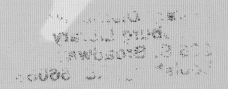

Contents

What Causes Oil Spills?

Oil is the world's main source of energy. It provides much of the vital electricity we use in homes and industry. We use it to power automobiles, trucks, ships, and planes. Oil is very valuable. It is also scarce, so oil companies now have to drill for it in remote places such as deserts, Arctic wastelands, and under the seabed.

Precious and deadly

Oil is precious. It can also be deadly. Drilling and transporting oil has led to some of the world's worst pollution disasters. Spills can happen at oil wells on land or on offshore rigs. When crude oil is tapped from the ground, it often shoots out with great force. A "blowout" happens if safety valves on the well fail, and escaping oil forms a "gusher." Black, sticky oil catches fire very easily, and then burns uncontrollably. There is a serious risk of an explosion.

An aerial view of an oil rig at sea.

Rescue boats attempt to put out a fire on board an oil tanker, and contain the oil that has been spilled.

What happens to spilled oil?

Spills also happen when oil is transported by ship, truck, or pipeline. Sixty percent of oil goes by sea, using tankers, which are the world's largest ships. Devastating spills result when tankers crash into rocks or other ships. The floating oil spreads out to form a slick. The impact is worst if the oil reaches the coast, where it kills wildlife and affects local people.

AT-A-GLANCE

Oil spills happen every year. If more than 750 tons escape, it is a major spill. As safety standards have improved, there have been fewer major spills.

Decade	Average number of major spills per year
1970s	25.4
1980s	9.3
1990s	7.9
2000s	3.3

What Can Be Done About Oil Spills?

When a major oil spill happens, emergency services swing into action. Every moment counts if lives are to be saved and environmental disaster avoided. The first step is to track the slick using aircraft or satellites. The impact will be reduced if the oil can be recovered at sea.

Dealing with slicks

Rescue ships use floating barriers called booms to contain the oil. Special ships suck or skim it from the surface and transport it to land for disposal. Oil can also be burned off, but this produces thick, poisonous black smoke, so it cannot be done near land.

Soldiers in protective suits sweep up oil following a major spill on a beach in South Korea, East Asia, in 2007.

Oil spilled at sea is eventually broken down by waves and weather. Tiny floating microbes break down oil droplets to form carbon dioxide and water. This takes time. Scientists sometimes mimic this natural process using chemicals called dispersants, which break the oil into tiny droplets.

EYEWITNESS

Emergency workers such as coastguard staff are trained to stay cool in a crisis. However, when lives are at stake, it's hard not to get involved. One officer said: "You think of the victims' families. It's impossible to separate yourself from the seriousness of the situation."

Damage to wildlife

If oil washes ashore, it can devastate wildlife. Seabirds and mammals such as seals have waterproof fur or feathers. If oil clogs the animal's fur or feathers, the waterproofing no longer works. The animal can die of cold. It can also swallow poisonous oil while trying to clean itself. Floating oil also kills tiny plants and animals called plankton, which provide food for many other creatures.

SAVING THE ENVIRONMENT

Rescue workers use booms and skimmers to contain and collect the oil. If it reaches the shore, workers use pumps, giant vacuum cleaners, or high-pressure hoses to remove it. Oil-covered animals may be saved by washing them with soapy water.

These cormorants are coated with oil spilled from a wrecked tanker called the *Prestige*.

Torrey Canyon, 1967

On March 18, 1967, at around 9 AM, the crew of the *Seven Stones Lightship* off Cornwall witnessed a slow-motion disaster. A massive oil tanker had drifted dangerously close to the razor-sharp reef nearby. The supertanker *Torrey Canyon* had taken a short cut through a narrow channel. Now the lightship crew watched helplessly as the ship ran aground on the reef.

The first major spill

Rescue boats failed to refloat the stricken tanker. Helicopters and lifeboats winched the crew to safety. After several days the enormous ship broke apart and its cargo, 110,000 tons of crude oil, began gushing into the sea.

BREAKING NEWS

March 29, 1967, England ...
Today, British Prime Minister Harold Wilson ordered RAF planes to bomb the stricken tanker *Torrey Canyon*, wrecked 11 days ago off Land's End, Cornwall. The RAF dropped 42 thousand-pound bombs and aircraft fuel to ignite the oil. However, many bombs missed their target, and high tides put out the flames.

The stricken oil tanker *Torrey Canyon*, beached on rocks off western Britain in 1967.

This was the world's first major oil spill. The British government had little idea how to deal with the disaster. RAF planes bombed the ship to sink it and burn off the oil, but did not succeed.

Huge slick

Crude oil spread out to form a 270 square-mile (700 sq km) slick. The seas were too rough for salvage boats to skim it off. The boats sprayed detergent to disperse the oil, but tides and currents drove the slick onto the coast.

Detergents are sprayed on the sea in Porthleven, Cornwall, to disperse the slick following the *Torrey Canyon* oil spill.

TEN YEARS ON

Oil from the *Torrey Canyon* polluted 160 miles (270 km) of coastline. Some beaches were covered by oil sludge a foot (30 cm) deep. Thousands of gallons of detergent were poured on the oil at sea and on the shore. However, the detergent was poisonous and killed thousands of seabirds. In the end, waves and weather broke up the oil. Ten years on, there was little trace of the disaster.

Amoco Cadiz, 1978

Shortly after 10 AM on March 16, 1978, ships in the English Channel picked up a distress call from the supertanker *Amoco Cadiz*. The fully laden tanker had been steaming toward the Netherlands when a severe storm damaged its rudder. Now it could no longer steer and was in grave danger of running onto Portsall Rocks, off France.

Rescue

Ships in the area responded to the call. A tug managed to fix a line to the stricken tanker. But in the evening, waves drove it onto the rocks. Oil gushed from the hull. Helicopters lifted the crew to safety during the night.

Pollution

The following morning the tanker broke in two and its entire cargo of 250,000 tons of oil poured into the sea. Oil mixed with water to form a sticky "mousse." By the end of April, winds and currents had driven the slick ashore to pollute 190 miles (320 km) of coastline. About 7,000 workers, mainly from the French Navy, painstakingly removed the oil using skimmers, hoses, pumps, and shovels.

Divers from the French Navy set up metal booms in an effort to contain the spilled oil at sea.

BREAKING NEWS

March 24, 1978,
Brittany, France ...

The French Navy is battling to deal with the huge oil slick from the *Amoco Cadiz*, wrecked off Portsall eight days ago. Efforts to recover the oil at sea failed due to stormy weather. Thirty ships in the area are spraying the slick with dispersants. Chalk is being used to sink the oil.

THREE YEARS ON

The *Amoco Cadiz* was the worst oil spill of its time. Two weeks after the accident, millions of dead fish, sea urchins, and mollusks washed ashore. Many had been killed by oil sunk by the chalk. More than 20,000 seabirds died. The French government ordered a detailed study of the impact. Three years later, rocky shores and beaches showed few traces of oil, but coastal marshes took longer to recover.

A rescue worker hoses down an oiled beach three months after the disaster. More than 130 beaches were harmed.

Tanker Collision, 1979

The helmsman of the supertanker *Aegean Captain* peered out through the lashing rain, but could see very little. The fully laden tanker was sailing through a narrow passage off the Caribbean island of Tobago on July 19, 1979 during a tropical storm. Suddenly there was a huge crash, followed by shouts of alarm from the bow. The ship was on fire—every tanker crew's worst nightmare.

Double trouble

Even worse news followed. The *Aegean Captain* had collided with another, even larger tanker, the *Atlantic Empress*. The second ship, also laden with oil, was soon ablaze. The crew of the *Aegean Captain* managed to douse the flames. The leaking tanker was towed to the island of Curacao, where its cargo was unloaded. The crew of the *Atlantic Empress* were not so lucky. The fire there blazed out of control and 26 sailors died.

Coastguard boats towed the burning ship out to sea, with crude oil gushing from its tanks. Firefighting ships aimed water cannons at the blaze but failed to put it out. Tugboats sprayed the flaming slick with dispersants.

Explosion

The fire raged for over a week. On July 29 a huge explosion rocked the ship, which began to list heavily. During the night of August 2 it sank, leaving a huge slick on the surface. With a total loss of 310,000 tons of oil, this was the world's worst tanker spill.

ONE YEAR ON

Tugboats followed the flaming slick left by the *Atlantic Empress*. Despite the scale of the disaster, very little pollution washed ashore. The slick had vanished by August 9. Experts believe that oil that did not burn off was broken down by waves, sunlight, and dispersants. No study was ever made of the impact on the open ocean or the seabed.

Black smoke billows from the damaged tanker *Atlantic Empress* following the collision in 1979.

AT-A-GLANCE

Date: July 19, 1979, 7 PM

Location: Caribbean, 10 miles (16 km) from Tobago

Names of vessels: *Atlantic Empress*, *Aegean Captain*

Cause of accident: Tanker collision

Death toll: 26 crew

Oil spilled: 310,000 tons

Impact: Slick dispersed out to sea

Piper Alpha Oil Rig Disaster, 1988

On July 6, 1988, at around 10 PM, a loud hiss of escaping gas was heard on the Piper Alpha oil platform in the North Sea. Moments later, the gas exploded and fire broke out. Crew in the rig's control room were killed by the explosion. Fire began to rage through the platform, fed by gas lines from two neighboring platforms.

A wall of flame prevented Piper Alpha workers from reaching lifeboats. The crew faced a stark choice—sheltering in the fire-damaged accommodations block, or leaping 100 feet (30 m) into a sea covered by burning oil.

Firefighters try to douse the flames on the Piper Alpha platform in 1988.

SAVING LIVES

A firefighting ship, the *Tharos*, was soon on the scene. Firefighters used water cannons to try to douse the flames. But the crew had to be careful—a direct hit from the powerful water jet could injure or even kill rig workers. In the end, intense heat forced the *Tharos* to retreat.

Rescue

The rig, with 224 workers, was located 115 miles (190 km) from Aberdeen in northeast Scotland. The Aberdeen Coastguard was alerted. Helicopters and rescue boats raced to the burning rig. Rescue craft lifted survivors from the water, but the flames were too intense for helicopters to land on the rig.

Terrible toll

Around 10:50 PM a second massive explosion rocked Piper Alpha. Shortly before midnight most of the platform collapsed into the sea. There was nothing more that the rescuers could do. A total of 167 people died in the world's worst offshore oil disaster. Two of the dead were crewmen from a rescue ship. Miraculously, there were 59 survivors.

An American team specializing in oil rig fires finally managed to put out the blaze.

THREE WEEKS ON

The Piper Alpha fire was put out three weeks later by a team led by US firefighter "Red" Adair. The team battled gale-force winds and 65 foot (20 m) waves. Later, a report concluded that the rig had been overcrowded and poorly maintained.

Exxon Valdez, 1989

The crewmen in the control room of the *Exxon Valdez* stared into the darkness, scanning for icebergs. It was shortly before midnight on March 24, 1989. The tanker had just left the Alaskan port of Valdez and was heading south with a full cargo of oil. The captain had ordered it out of normal shipping lanes to avoid icebergs. Now the third mate checked the radar and saw the tanker was close to a reef. Moments later there was a sickening crash. The ship had run aground.

EYEWITNESS

Chief mate James Kunkel was roused by the crash. He raced to the control room where he found the captain trying to maneuver the tanker off the reef. It was now listing heavily, with oil gushing from a gaping hole. Kunkel reported: "I feared for my life." He told the captain the ship would capsize if he managed to get it off the reef. Salvage experts later confirmed the boat would have gone down if freed. Luckily it got wedged on a narrow shelf.

BREAKING NEWS

March 24, 1989, Alaska …
Reports are coming in of an oil tanker accident in Alaska. The *Exxon Valdez* has been wrecked on Bligh Reef in Prince William Sound. The ship is owned by ExxonMobil. Scientists fear the spilled oil will spell disaster for seabirds, whales, seals, and sea otters that inhabit these remote waters.

Worst spill

The captain radioed the authorities. A coastguard plane dropped booms, pumps, and oil recovery gear for local ships to use. Salvage crews were able to pump the oil left in the ship's tanks onto other craft. However, 46,000 tons of oil had been spilled—the worst tanker spill in US history.

Oil pours from the *Exxon Valdez* as it lies wedged on a rocky reef in Prince William Sound in 1989.

AT-A-GLANCE

Date: March 24, 1989, midnight
Location: Prince William Sound, Alaska
Name of vessel: *Exxon Valdez*
Cause of accident: Tanker ran aground
Death toll: None
Oil spilled: 40,000 tons
Impact: Slick polluted 1,200 miles
(1,900 km) of coastline

Exxon Valdez: The Impact

Within 48 hours of the accident, oil company ExxonMobil had organized a fleet of 60 ships to suck up the spilled oil. However, the oil had meanwhile mixed with water to form a thick "mousse" that was too heavy to suck up—a serious setback.

Coastal devastation

While experts argued about whether to use chemical dispersants, nature took control. Hurricane-force winds swept the slick over booms and southward to Kodiak Island and beyond. The oil then washed ashore to coat 1,200 miles (1,900 km) of wild coastline, including beaches, islands, and reserves.

The impact was devastating. Thick, black oil killed 250,000 seabirds and 2,800 sea otters. Fish such as salmon and herring were badly affected, along with eagles and bears in local forests.

SAVING THE ENVIRONMENT

Scientists used an unusual technique to clear oil from the worst-affected beaches. They sprayed the shore with fertilizer to encourage the growth of oil-eating microbes. The experiment paid off. The sprayed beaches showed a marked improvement in just two to three weeks.

Workers spray hot water on oil-covered beaches in Prince William Sound, Alaska.

Clean-up

An army of 11,000 workers was soon at work on the coast, using high-pressure hoses and absorbent materials to remove oil. Skimmer ships worked offshore. Hundreds of oil-coated animals were washed at emergency centers. However, workers only managed to save a small fraction of the stricken animals.

Rescuers clean oil from a harbor seal following the *Exxon Valdez* spill.

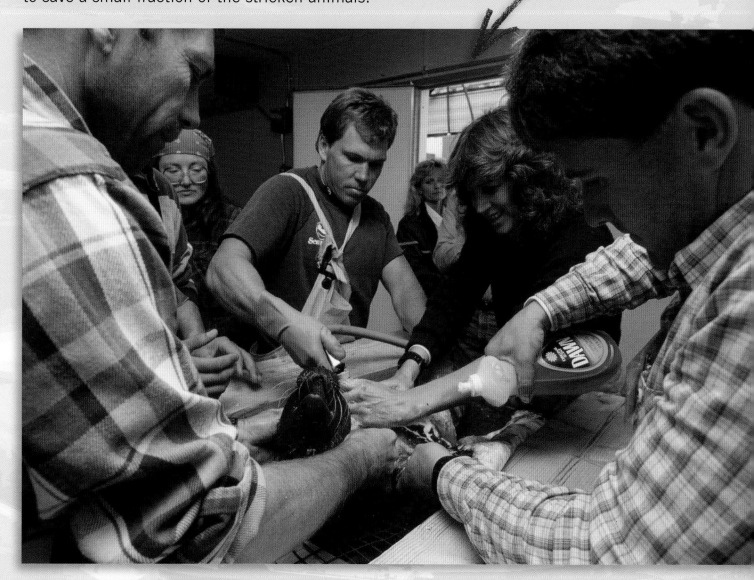

TWENTY YEARS ON

ExxonMobil spent more than US$1 billion on the cleanup. Twenty years on, some pollution could still be seen. Experts believe it will be another ten years before all the oil disappears. Some of the money paid by ExxonMobil has been used to enlarge a national park.

Gulf War, 1991

The world's worst oil spill was caused deliberately (not by accident). In 1990, war broke out in the Persian Gulf when Iraqi dictator Saddam Hussein invaded the oil-rich state of Kuwait. The United States and its allies supported Kuwait and drove Iraq out. In 1991, retreating Iraqi forces set fire to Kuwait's oil fields. They also turned on the faucets at oil terminals on the Gulf coast to create a giant slick.

Smoke and flames

The effects were devastating. US troops found hundreds of oil wells burning uncontrollably. Choking black smoke filled the air. The slick in the Gulf covered 3,800 square miles (10,000 sq km). The US government called in famed firefighter "Red" Adair to put out the well fires. Red assessed the situation and requested cranes, bulldozers, and other equipment.

SAVING THE ENVIRONMENT

Booms, skimmer ships, and chemicals helped with the cleanup work at sea. In the end, nature lent a hand. Oil-eating microbes occur naturally in these oil-rich waters. They multiplied rapidly and ate the largest spill on Earth.

Toward the end of the Gulf War, Iraqi dictator Saddam Hussein ordered his soldiers to set fire to Kuwait's oil wells.

Putting out the fires

Red's teams reached Kuwait in March 1991. A lot of water would obviously be needed to put out the well fires, but water was scarce in this desert land. Pipelines normally used to transport oil to the coast were reversed to bring seawater to the flames.

EYEWITNESS

When tackling well fires, Red Adair believed the greatest danger was when the fire was actually out. "As long as the well is blowing, there is a possibility the well could reignite, injuring or killing everyone on location."

The firefighters worked systematically. As they tackled one fire, soldiers restored roads and pipelines to the next. Experts had estimated it would take three to five years to extinguish more than 600 fires. Red's team managed it in nine months, and not a single man was lost.

Firefighters from many countries worked together to put out the burning oil wells of Kuwait. They succeeded in record time.

Sea Empress, 1996

On February 15, 1996, the Port Authority of Milford Haven in South Wales received an emergency call from the oil tanker *Sea Empress*. The ship, carrying 143,000 tons of crude oil, had been heading for the oil refinery at Milford Haven. But strong currents pulled it onto rocks around 8 PM. Oil was pouring from the ship.

BREAKING NEWS

February 15, 1996, 9:18 PM, South Wales ...

An emergency is unfolding on the Welsh coast. The supertanker *Sea Empress* has run aground off Pembrokeshire. The first news of the disaster came from local people who reported a strong smell of oil in the air. Spilled oil threatens the beautiful Pembrokeshire coastline, a national park with several island reserves. There are fears for local fishing and tourist industries.

Tugs to the rescue

Tugs were quickly on the scene. They fixed lines to the beached tanker and hauled it off the rocks, only for the ship to ground again within minutes. Each time, jagged rocks tore at the ship's hull, increasing the oil spill. After nearly a week, the tanker was finally refloated and towed away. Some 63,000 tons of oil were recovered from its tanks, but 80,000 tons had been spilled.

The stricken *Sea Empress* on the rocks off Milford Haven, South Wales, in February 1996. The fully laden tanker had almost reached port when disaster struck.

Cleaning up

The effort to recover the oil at sea was partly successful. Booms contained the slick while it was pumped into rescue vessels. Tides, the weather, and chemicals helped to disperse the oil. But a large slick made its way ashore. More than 1,000 workers cleaned local beaches using hoses, skimmers, and sponges.

Workers at a wildlife rescue center in South Wales use soapy water to clean oil from a scoter duck caught in the *Sea Empress* spill.

SAVING ANIMALS

Puffins, cormorants, and other seabirds breed on the Pembrokeshire coast. A special rescue center was set up to clean oil-covered birds. Unfortunately 70 percent died within a few weeks of treatment. Experts said the impact would have been worse had the spill happened later in spring, when many more birds arrive to breed.

Deepwater Horizon, 2010

On the night of April 20, 2010, all seemed well aboard the oil rig Deepwater Horizon in the Gulf of Mexico. Many of the 126 crew were asleep. The rig was a modern, semisubmersible platform designed to drill new wells on the seabed. It had just finished drilling a well 35 miles (60 km) off Louisiana. A temporary cap had been put on the well, which was linked to the floating rig by a long riser pipe.

Explosion

At 10 PM the crew were roused by a violent explosion. Gas had surged up the pipe despite two concrete plugs and a safety valve called a blowout preventer. Rig worker Chris Choy was woken by the blast. "I could see the sea on fire. The walkway above me was on fire. As soon as I saw the flames I knew there was no way we were going to put it out." Many of the crew abandoned the rig in a lifeboat. Those left aboard had little choice but to leap into the flaming sea.

RESCUE!

Oil worker Mike Williams was still on Deepwater when the lifeboat left. He leapt from the rig and hit the water with a smack, only to surface in burning oil. Williams kicked and swam away with all his strength. Eventually he heard a faint voice calling "Over here!" Moments later he was hauled into a small rescue boat.

Firefighting ships spray the blazing oil rig Deepwater Horizon on April 21, 2010, in an effort to damp down the flames. Meanwhile coastguard helicopters search for survivors.

Coastguard alerted

News of the disaster reached the US Coastguard. Helicopters were in the air in minutes. The pilots could see a column of flame lighting up the night sky. One said: "It was like flying into New York City." Coastguard swimmers helped survivors onto boats. Injured workers were flown to hospital. All the while, the fire raged out of control.

BREAKING NEWS

April 21, 2010, 8 AM, Louisiana ...

The US Coastguard is frantically searching for survivors after an explosion on an oil rig in the Gulf of Mexico. The rig is operated by the oil company BP. Eleven workers are missing and 17 are badly injured. Support ships are spraying the rig with water to cool it until firefighting vessels arrive.

Deepwater Horizon: The Impact

On the morning of April 22, 36 hours after the explosion, Deepwater Horizon was still burning. The steel structure was now buckling under the intense heat. Around 10 AM, after more explosions, the rig began to tilt. Then it slid beneath the waves, leaving oil burning on the surface.

Damaged wellhead

As the rig collapsed, the pipe connecting it to the well on the seabed broke. Oil began to gush from the damaged wellhead. It soon formed a massive slick on the surface. The rig's operator, BP, tried to seal the wellhead using remote-operated submersibles, but without success.

EYEWITNESS

Salvage expert James Wait watched the final moments of Deepwater Horizon. "We could hear a creaking, groaning and settling. There were multiple explosions. Just listening to the rig, you were listening to a ship dying. By 10:22 she was gone."

A US Coastguard boat contains spilled oil from Deepwater Horizon inside a boom. The oil will then be pumped into the ship.

Cleaning the sea and coast

By the end of May the slick covered 2,500 square miles (6,500 sq km). Through June and July, 6,000 ships and 100 aircraft worked to reduce the slick by dispersing it, skimming off oil or burning it at sea. Meanwhile, thousands of workers used booms and skimmers to keep oil away from beaches and wetlands. They rescued oil-covered seabirds, turtles, and other wildlife.

SAVING THE ENVIRONMENT

A coastguard boat called the *Oak* was on the scene soon after oil began to surface. The skimming ship is fitted with a powerful pump to suck up oil. The oil is transferred to a salvage boat. In the first four weeks after the disaster, the *Oak* recovered 277,000 gallons (1 million liters) of oil.

Sealing the leak

In mid-July, BP announced that it had managed to seal the well with a temporary cap. It was also digging two relief wells to permanently seal the leak. Experts rate the Gulf spill as the worst in US history. Local fisheries and tourism have been devastated. The impact will be felt for many years to come.

A giant slick of liquid crude oil and oil clotted by dispersants floats on the surface of the Gulf of Mexico on May 6, 2010.

Avoiding Oil Spills

Safety standards in the oil industry have improved in the last 20 years. There have been far fewer major spills. However, disasters such as Deepwater Horizon still happen from time to time. So what can be done to prevent future spills?

Safer ships

Oil tanker design has improved since the 1970s. All new tankers have a double hull. If the outer layer gets damaged, the inner hull still holds its cargo. However, these huge ships are very difficult to maneuver. Some 30 million barrels of oil are at sea at any time, supplying the world's energy needs. That's enough to fill 2,000 Olympic swimming pools. With so much oil on the move, tanker spills will always happen, thanks to human error, storms, and reefs.

Safer rigs and wells

Safety at oil rigs and wells has improved since the Piper Alpha disaster. Rig workers now sometimes sleep in ships called flotels (floating hotels), away from the rig. Maintenance workers and divers regularly check every part of the rig. However, drilling accidents still happen, especially when oil companies try to cut costs.

Polluter pays

Cleaning up a major spill is incredibly expensive. In 2010, BP set aside US$20 billion for the cleanup. Since the 1980s, new laws have required companies that cause pollution to fund the cleanup. This is called "polluter pays." In future, oil companies may become even more safety conscious, because the penalties are so high.

Modern tankers, such as the Saudi Arabian *Sirius Star*, have a double hull to reduce the possibility of an oil spill.

The search for oil

Oil is becoming scarce. That's why oil companies are drilling in ever more remote places, such as the deep ocean. However, we need to be sure we have the technology to drill safely in such locations. In May 2010, the United States announced a temporary ban on new deepwater wells.

Glossary

absorbent Describes a material that soaks up liquid. Such materials are called absorbents.

blowout An uncontrolled release of oil or gas from an oil well.

boom A floating barrier used to contain spilled oil.

bow The front of a ship.

capsize (Of a boat) overturn in the water.

crude oil Oil when it comes out of the ground, before it is refined.

dispersant A chemical used to disperse or break down oil.

disperse (Of a substance) break down or spread over a wide area.

douse Pour liquid over, to extinguish (a fire).

environment The surroundings in which we live.

evaporate (Of a liquid) change into a gas.

flotel Floating accommodation, sometimes used by oil rig workers.

fuel A substance that gives off energy when burned.

gusher A fountain of oil that erupts from a well when safety valves are breached.

hull The body of a ship.

ignite Set light to something.

list Tilt to one side (describing a damaged ship).

microbes Tiny living things that are too small to see without a microscope. Some microbes feed on oil and break it down.

mousse The name given to the thick mixture that forms when oil combines with seawater.

multiply Breed rapidly.

oil refinery A factory where crude oil is processed to make fuel and other products.

oil rig A drilling platform that taps undersea oil.

plankton Microscopic plants and animals that float on water and provide food for many animals.

pollutant A substance that harms the air, water, or land.

pollution Any harmful substance that damages the environment.

radar Equipment used to detect objects by bouncing radio waves off them.

refine (Of a substance) process to make pure.

rudder The oarlike structure used to steer a ship.

salvage Rescue something, particularly from a wrecked or damaged ship.

semisubmersible A vehicle designed to operate partly underwater.

slick A thin layer of oil floating on a large area of water.

submersible An underwater vehicle, or submarine.

winch A lifting device consisting of a rope or cable winding around a horizontal rotating drum.

Further Information

Books

The BP Oil Spill (True Books) by Peter Benoit (Children's Press, 2011)

The Exxon Valdez's Deadly Oil Spill by Linda Ward Beech (Bearport Publishing, 2007)

The Great Penguin Rescue: 40,000 Penguins, a Devastating Oil Spill, and the Inspiring Story of the World's Largest Animal Rescue by Dyan DeNapoli (Free Press, 2010)

Oil Spill: Disaster by Scholastic editors (Scholastic, 2010)

Oil Spills by Peggy J. Parks (KidHaven Press, 2005)

Web Sites

www.awesomestories.com/disasters/deepwater-horizon
This web site has an exciting account of the Gulf of Mexico oil spill.

www.itopf.com/information-services/data-and-statistics/statistics/
Information and statistics about major oil spills from the International Tanker Owners Pollution Federation.

library.thinkquest.org/CRO215471/oil_spills.htm
Information about oil spills.

science.howstuffworks.com/environmental/green-science/cleaning-oil-spill.htm
Information about cleaning up oil spills.

seawifs.gsfc.nasa.gov/OCEAN_PLANET/HTML/peril_oil_pollution.html
Smithsonian Institution web page on oil pollution.

Index